Passwords & Internet Addresses Journal

FOR DUMMIES®

A Wiley Brand

by Ryan C. Williams

with
Michael J. Arata, Jr.
Kevin Beaver
Chris Botello
Marsha Collier
Ray Everett-Church
Laura Fitton
Michael C. Gruen
John R. Levine
Leslie Poston
Andy Rathbone
Doug Sahlin
Greg Stebben
Eric Tyson
Margaret Levine Young

FOR DUMMIES®
A Wiley Brand

Passwords & Internet Addresses Journal For Dummies®

Published by: **John Wiley & Sons, Inc.,** 111 River Street, Hoboken, NJ 07030-5774, www.wiley.com

Copyright © 2014 by John Wiley & Sons, Inc., Hoboken, New Jersey

Published simultaneously in Canada

For general information on our other products and services, please contact our Customer Care Department within the U.S. at 877-762-2974, outside the U.S. at 317-572-3993, or fax 317-572-4002. For technical support, please visit www.wiley.com/techsupport.

Wiley publishes in a variety of print and electronic formats and by print-on-demand. Some material included with standard print versions of this book may not be included in e-books or in print-on-demand. If this book refers to media such as a CD or DVD that is not included in the version you purchased, you may download this material at http://booksupport.wiley.com. For more information about Wiley products, visit www.wiley.com.

Library of Congress Control Number: 2013950464

ISBN: 978-1-118-82836-6

Manufactured in the United States of America

10 9 8 7 6 5 4 3 2 1

Contents at a Glance

Table of Contents

Introduction

*A*t some point, everybody interacts with a password. Whether you're quickly shuffling between your e-mail, social media, and banking accounts while chatting via some form of instant messenger or just using an ATM for a little extra cash, you inevitably must provide a small bit of information to get access to your larger amount of information. And that's why you have to keep those small bits of information (here and after known as *passwords*) as secure as possible. This book shows you the best, most effective ways to secure your passwords while keeping the rest of your digital life safe as well.

About This Book

You probably encounter just as much misinformation about your passwords as there are passwords in the world. Without delving too deeply into technical jargon, I clear up that misinformation and give you a clear, descriptive guide to password safety. And, in true *For Dummies* style, you can get whatever information you need as quickly as possible!

This book also includes a passwords journal, which you can use to log your usernames, passwords, security questions and answers, and other account information. Be sure to check out the preface to the journal. It lists every type of password-protected account that I can think of, and you might be surprised when you realize how many password-protected accounts you have.

If a password journal isn't your style, you can instead use the password quick reference at the back of the book. Here, you can keep usernames and passwords for your most often used accounts.

If you do choose to write your passwords in this book, keep it in a very secure place. Seriously, consider storing the book in a lock-and-key location, or at least in a safe place at home. You don't want to leave this book lying around in a bar or something.

However you'd like to use this book is up to you! Read the chapters from start to finish, or just go to the section you need to learn about first. Or flip to the journal or quick reference and start logging passwords.

When you're reading through this book, keep these things in mind:

✔ When I talk about terms for the first time, those terms appear in *italics*. Take note of these terms, because you'll probably encounter them quite a bit throughout the text.

✔ Any web addresses will appear like this — www.dummies. com. You can't copy and paste these addresses from a paper book, obviously, but this presentation lets you know what to type in your browser window. I'll keep the addresses short, too. I promise.

Foolish Assumptions

If you took the time to pick up this book and read this far, it's probably safe to assume you use the Internet at least occasionally to send e-mail, check your Facebook account, or manage a bank account. It really doesn't matter how often you do it — just the fact that you're on the Internet makes passwords a good topic to address. Beyond that, this book presents information that applies to newbies and power users alike. Don't feel left out — everybody needs to be secure!

Icons Used in This Book

 The Tip icons mark tips (duh!) and shortcuts that help you create effective and secure passwords. You don't *have* to read them, but you're already there, so why not check them out?

 Important information bears repeating. The Remember icons ensure that these vital points stick with you, even after you've finished the book.

 This whole book may sound a little like a warning, but the Warning icons really let you know when the sirens start flashing. Pay close attention to save yourself some trouble later.

Where to Go from Here

You can always start from the beginning if you feel like it, but there's no reason you can't jump into a different section if you're feeling especially curious. Just jump in and start learning!

Part I
Getting Started with Passwords

In this part . . .

Passwords protect our most sensitive online information, and most people now have multiple online accounts. In this part, I cover the most important safety practices for online accounts so that you can shop, bank, and network online securely.

Chapter 1

Safeguarding Your Identity

. . . .

In This Chapter

▶ Evaluating your private information and where it is online

▶ Keeping your private information out of the wrong hands

▶ Taking swift and effective action if your identity is stolen

. . . .

*I*t's easier and easier to share information about yourself online these days, whether you're active in social media or online shopping. Overall, this book helps you create and guard your passwords for online activity, but this chapter specifically helps you understand the kind of information that you're asked to share online and the potential ramifications that can occur if that information falls into the wrong hands. Consider this chapter the explanation of why you should create strong and safe passwords — you want to keep personal information like this away from others.

Assessing Your Information

To get started, take stock of what kind of information you have out there on the Internet and what kind of risk it poses if it's stolen. Unless you're off the grid in the Montana woods or working with extremely secure biometric sensors on a top-secret government project, you deal with passwords every day.

Where do I use passwords?

The easy answer is: everywhere. It seems like everything online requires a password of some sort. The questions you should ask are: How long do I make the password? What characters do I include in that password? Should I use a password or a passphrase? From accessing your computer to getting your e-mail to viewing your bank records, you identify yourself with a password.

Figuring out what information is sensitive

More than likely, your sensitive information involves numbers. We live in a world where numbers mean everything. You use phone numbers to reach others, you enter credit card numbers to buy your favorite products online, and you hand over your date of birth, Social Security Number, and other hugely important digits any time you apply for a job or a bank loan. Companies use employee and medical record numbers for identification and record keeping, and these pieces of *personally identifiable information* (PII) are keys to your identity on the phone, online, or in writing.

The vulnerable personal information that identity thieves use is as follows:

- ✓ **Social Security Number (SSN):** This is, of course, the nine-digit personal identification number (compliments of the federal government) that everyone needs to get a job, pay taxes, and apply for credit. The SSN is the key to the *kingdom* — financial kingdom, that is. The identity thief uses your SSN to apply for credit, file false tax returns, get a job, open bank accounts, and so on.

- ✓ **Date of birth (DOB):** A DOB is a piece of the personal information puzzle, but if an identity thief has this piece by itself, it's not a problem. When the thief uses your DOB in conjunction with your SSN, she can become you.

- ✓ **Security questions:** You see these questions — such as what was your first pet's name and where did you go to high school — when you're setting up an online account. There's no right answer to these questions, though; they're just prompts for an answer the system can use to identify you.

- ✓ **Mother's maiden name:** This name is used to verify your identity when accessing financial information. Identity thieves use your mother's maiden name to verify their identity as yours to access your financial records and open new accounts in your name.

Security questions have begun to include a father's middle name as well. Everybody gets equal time!

- **Personal identification numbers (PINs):** These are usually four- (or more) digit numbers used to access your bank accounts online or when using your ATM card.

- **Passwords:** Your passwords are the keys to any information stored electronically. When an identity thief has the password to an account, that thief has complete access to the contents of that account, whether it's a bank account (your money), an e-mail account (your personal information), or your Netflix account (your potentially bad taste in movies).

- **Driver's license number:** This number used to identify you is printed on your license. When the identity thief has your driver's license number, she can have a phony license made that shows your name and driver's license number with her picture.

Beyond numbers, though, you can still provide a great deal more personal information. Social media can let people know where you live, where you went to school, your likes and dislikes, and other information that people can use to get a complete picture of who you are. Think about all of the information you've distributed on these networks (both old and new — hello MySpace and Friendster!) and how likely it is that somebody could turn up this information through a quick Google search. Even if you deactivate or delete your account, that information can still be accessible through cached searches and archives.

By using your personal information, identity thieves can party hard on your nickel and good credit reputation. They spend like there's no tomorrow because they know that someone else (you) is picking up the tab. Identity thieves can use your personal information to open accounts, such as a cellphone account, in your name. Of course, they don't pay the bills and continue to use the phone until you discover the theft and the heat is on; then they drop that account and move on to another unsuspecting victim.

Avoiding Identity Theft and Fraud

The easiest way to do this is never tell anybody anything. A pair of glasses and a cape might be helpful as well.

Seriously, though, you're going to have to share some information if you wish to interact on the Internet at all. So you're not looking for a secret identity as much as you are a trusted and limited identity. You want to share only the necessary information with only those who really need it. So maybe you're okay with giving your full name to a social network, but not to a site you've never heard of before. And you're okay with putting a PIN into a banking website, but you certainly wouldn't post it on that social network.

Give only the minimum information necessary to any online source, and make sure you know who's receiving the information.

Avoiding phishermen

The U.S. Federal Trade Commission (www.ftc.gov/idtheft) offers this advice to prevent identity theft: First, look out for *phishing,* or e-mails that claim to come from a bank or another online account, such as eBay, and claims that your account has a problem that you can clean up by clicking a link in the message. (I tell you more about phishing scams in Chapter 3.) These messages are never real, but they're extremely dangerous. If your bank thinks that a security problem exists, it doesn't tell you by e-mail. If you aren't sure, contact the company by phone or type its web address (for example, www. *yourbank*.com) into your browser by hand and look for the customer service section.

Make sure that your family knows this rule well: Never, *never,* **never** enter passwords, credit card numbers, or other personal information at a web page you opened by clicking a link in an e-mail.

Phishers have gotten a lot more skillful since the earliest phishes a decade ago, and now often have good editors and use a spell checker, so you can't rely on spelling and grammar mistakes, although they're dead giveaways when you spot them. Here are a few additional tips:

- ✔ Assume that every e-mail that leads you to a page seeking passwords or credit card numbers or other personal information is a phishing expedition.

- ✔ If the e-mail purports to be from a company you've never heard of, ignore it.

✔ If the message says that it's from a company with whom you have an account, go to the company's website by typing the company's URL into your browser, *not* by clicking a link in the e-mail. When you get to the company's website, look for the My Account link. If there's a problem, when you log in, you should see a notice. If there's no way to log in and you're still concerned, forward a copy of the e-mail to the customer service department or pick up the phone and call the number on your card or monthly statement.

One trick phishers use to fool Internet users is *website spoofing* — tricking your browser into displaying one address when you're actually at another site. Some browsers allow a website to show only its main address so that it doesn't look so geeky. Phishers take advantage of this capability. Better web browsers offer protection against website spoofing — they always show the actual web address of the page you're on.

Protecting your privacy

Before posting information on a social networking site like Facebook or Google+, carefully review your privacy settings. These sites give the impression that the information you provide is visible only to your close friends, but it ain't necessarily so.

When posting information that appears on a public website (other than your own, or your social networking sites) or in any discussion venue, don't use your full name. This advice doesn't apply if you're working in a business context, such as posting information on your company's website.

Never provide your name, address, or phone number to someone you don't know.

Never believe anyone who says that he's from Facebook tech support, eBay fraud prevention, PayPal administration, or a similar-sounding authority and asks you for your password. No legitimate entity will ever ask you for your password.

Be especially careful about disclosing information about kids. Don't fill out profiles that ask for a kid's name, hometown, school, age, address, or phone number, because they're invariably used for "targeted marketing" (also known as junk mail).

Privacy Pests and How to Deal with Them

So if you control who accesses your information, how is it that people still find a way to creep into your online life and ask you for more? Let's take a look at the most common ways to access details about you on the Internet.

How do pests obtain your info?

Here you are, still sitting quietly in a chair and reading this book about passwords. Can you begin to hear the faint scratches of the privacy pests as they claw away at the walls of your electronic security?

No? Then it's time to start looking in some of the mustier corners of your daily activities to see whether you can see any telltale signs. As an example, look at an everyday action, like buying a book (this book!). Did you buy this book

- ✓ **Over the Internet?** Did the website ask you for any personally identifiable information — your mailing address perhaps, or an e-mail address? By buying the book over the Internet, you revealed some information about yourself to the bookseller. As you continue to read this book, someone at the site may be adding that information to all the other personal data that's already been collected about you based on all the other things you've purchased — or even just looked at — while on that website.

- ✓ **While browsing the web at home?** If so, you may have revealed to your Internet Service Provider some information about yourself, including your interests and purchasing habits. As you continue reading, someone may be adding that information to all the other personal data that's already been collected about you based on all the places you've surfed and the things you've bought online.

- ✓ **While browsing the web at work?** If so, you may have revealed to your employer some information about yourself. Luckily, you weren't looking for job-hunting books. Oops! You *were* looking for those, too? Whatever the case, someone may be adding that information to your personnel file now, along with all the other personal data that's already been collected about you because your employer has the legal right to monitor you and record every move you make on the Internet while you're at work.

✔ **Using an insecure Internet browser?** If so, you may have revealed some information about yourself to a hacker in a faraway place who may have already targeted you as the one whose credit card number will buy him a new video game system — or maybe even a wardrobe or new car. While you're reading now, he may be busy collecting additional information and building an intimate profile of you that he can use to fraudulently spend your money, online and offline.

Follow these steps to help reduce your privacy concerns:

✔ **Don't submit your personal information on computers you don't own.** This includes your work computer. If you don't want people seeing what you're typing or viewing on the Internet, restrict your activity to your own computer. Your boss will probably be happier that way, too.

✔ **Set your web browser to private browsing.** Chrome may call it something different from Firefox, but the gist of the function is that the browser doesn't store cookies or track browser history while in this mode. You may forego some of the convenience of browsing the web, but you do gain a measure of privacy. You can also turn on Do Not Track, a relatively new browsing feature that keeps companies from tracking your Internet activity via cookies. Not all browsers support this function yet, but Firefox has taken the lead in providing Do Not Track to users.

✔ **Don't give out personal information, including your e-mail address.** Even if you're trying to win a fabulous prize, be aware that the company running the contest wants your personal information to better track and market to you. Opt out of any mailings, and maybe even use a dedicated e-mail account for the spam you'll likely receive if the lure of the prize is too great.

What to look for in privacy policies

Have you ever seen the magicians Penn & Teller vow never to show you how their magic tricks are done — and then play the old shell game with a small ball hidden under one of three clear plastic cups so that you can see exactly how they perform the trick?

I am about to perform the privacy lawyer's equivalent of that trick by showing you what you should look for in a privacy statement as though you were reading it through the clear plastic lenses of the sneakiest, most cynical lawyer in town. Ask yourself whether a website's privacy policy tells you

✔ **Explicitly what information the website is collecting.** Is the site getting your name and address? Your e-mail address? The IP address of your computer? Your credit card number? The combination to your gym locker or to the hidden safe in the den? If the site doesn't say exactly what information it's collecting, you should assume the worst.

✔ **How and from where the site is collecting your information.** Does the site use an order form to collect data? Is it buying databases from other advertisers? Is it searching public records down at the county courthouse? Is it paying some nasty-looking guy to tail you? You should know from where the site is getting information about you because the amount of information it's gathering should be appropriate to the service you're getting. A website that's selling you a new flamingo for your front lawn doesn't need to know as much about you as an online mortgage banker does when you're shopping for a home loan.

✔ **How your information will be used.** Here's where the worst advertising-speak usually happens. You have to read carefully and be deeply skeptical to figure out what the site is saying because everything it says emphasizes how exciting and wonderful the site's services are and how thrilled you will be with all the benefits it provides because you're so willing to share your personal information. Will the site customize or personalize its content for you the next time you visit? Will it drive you crazy by sending you catalogs by snail mail and e-mailing you ads by the dozens? Will it sell your personal information to other advertisers? Will it call you at home every week during the last five minutes of *The Simpsons?* If you're already sick of all the junk mail and spam and phone calls, you need to know this information to decide whether you want to have anything more to do with these sites.

✔ **Whether and how you can make the site stop collecting information about you.** If you don't want a company to collect information about you, either it can give you a chance to object, or you can take your business elsewhere. Some places would rather annoy you and drive you to their competition than give you a chance to make your feelings known. If a site's policy doesn't tell you how to stop the data collection, take that as an invitation to visit the competition.

✔ **How to see what information about you it already has and how to delete it or correct it if it's wrong.** On an episode of the TV show *Friends,* Chandler Bing receives *TV Guide* addressed to a "Miss Chanandler Bong." If Chandler knew how to correct his information, you wouldn't have plot points from a sitcom inflicted on you in a book about Internet privacy.

✔ **How the site protects your information.** Does the site use encryption to keep bad guys from snatching your personal information as it passes between your computer and its own? Does it have security measures in place to keep people from stealing your information from its databases? Sites are sometimes vague about specific security measures, and that's a good thing. Providing too many specifics gives crooks an edge, and the unknown keeps them guessing. If the site's policy fails to mention security or doesn't assert that it's using industry best practices or some other silver-tongued phrase to reassure you that it's protecting your data, your privacy and security may be the last thing on its list.

✔ **Who is responsible for making sure that the site lives up to its promises.** Many e-commerce firms have appointed chief privacy officers and other dedicated personnel to manage their consumer information practices and to be the point person in ensuring that all promises made in a privacy policy are honored. If a site's policy doesn't say who has responsibility for overseeing the privacy of your data, you're better off assuming that the answer is nobody.

You'll also want to review the privacy policies for the apps you use on your smart device of choice. Make sure you look at the settings for all of the apps you use and see how they want to use your information. Scrupulous developers ask you for your permission (usually in an alert where you must click

Yes or No) to use your information or to gain access to contact information on your phone, but not all app developers may be as scrupulous. Check all the settings for an app, and don't be afraid to delete apps that don't play by the rules. Plenty more apps will be available to take their place.

Responding to Identity Theft or Fraud

If identity theft happens to you, act immediately!

✔ After you identify which accounts have been compromised, contact those providers immediately.

✔ Contact the three major credit bureaus (Equifax, Experian, and TransUnion).

- You can find contact information for these organizations at www.consumer.ftc.gov/articles/0155-free-credit-reports.

- Tell each bureau that you're the victim of identity theft and report your ID as stolen. Because you're the victim of identity theft, the three bureaus will each give you a copy of your credit report for free.

- Ask all three credit bureaus to flag your file with a fraud alert and add a victim's statement to your file. This statement can be as simple as "Someone is using my ID to fraudulently apply for credit. Before new accounts can be opened, I must be contacted at *<your phone number>*."

- Ask all three credit bureaus to tell you the names and phone numbers of all creditors with whom fraudulent accounts have been opened. Contact each of these creditors to report the identity theft.

- Ask each credit bureau to clear your file of all inquiries that have been generated as a result of the fraudulent use of your information.

- Be sure to request and check your credit reports every few months to watch for new incidents of fraud.

- ✔ Report the identity theft to your local law enforcement agency. Insist on filing a written report.

- ✔ Monitor all other financial records (incoming mail, phone bills, credit card bills, and bank statements, for example) for signs of other fraud.

For the most up-to-date information on how to protect yourself against identity theft or what to do if it happens to you, visit `www.privacyrights.org` and `www.consumer.ftc.gov/features/feature-0014-identity-theft`.

You aren't alone in the fight against identity theft. From the federal government and credit card companies to your local police, your allies abound and can help you with many aspects of identity theft. Here are some of your key sources of help:

- ✔ **The Federal Trade Commission (FTC):** The FTC provides information useful for preventing identity theft and knowing what to do if you're a victim. Its website (`www.consumer.gov/idtheft`) is chock-full of statistics, information, forms, and more to help you understand and prevent identity theft as well as what to do if you're a victim. When you file a complaint online, the report is forwarded to law enforcement as well.

- ✔ **The Social Security Administration (SSA):** The SSA has guidelines for reporting fraud on its website (`www.ssa.gov`). Also, you need to submit a fraud-reporting form to the SSA Office of Inspector General (OIG), an investigative branch. The SSA recommends downloading the form, completing it, and then sending it via fax or regular mail to ensure confidentiality. When you report the use of your SSN for identity theft, the SSA will not investigate the identity theft but will look into benefit fraud. The SSA will not issue a new SSN if you have been the victim of identity theft.

- ✔ **Most local law enforcement agencies:** These agencies provide information on how to prevent identity theft and what to do if you become a victim.

- ✔ **Federal law enforcement agencies:** The most active federal law enforcement agencies investigating ID theft are the U.S. Postal Inspection Service and the U.S. Secret Service.

- **Internet Crime Complaint Center (IC3):** The IC3 (www. ic3.gov) is a partnership among the FBI and the National White Collar Crime Center (NW3C). At the website, you can file a complaint and read about recent scams and other news. The IC3 reports the complaints to the proper local authorities.

- **Federal Bureau of Investigation (FBI):** Go to www.fbi. gov/scams-safety to find more information.

- **Financial institutions and credit card companies:** Most financial institutions provide tips about preventing fraud and knowing what to do if you're a victim. Some institutions provide discounts and links to sites that charge an annual membership fee for providing identity theft protection. For example, I subscribe to a CreditExpert.com service, and the site is part of the credit bureau Experian.

  To help stem the upward trend of credit card fraud, the card-issuing companies monitor and look for irregular patterns of use. The credit card companies monitor what you charge on a monthly basis, and when something varies from the typical pattern, the card company calls and asks whether you made the purchase. For example, when people go on vacation and don't notify the card company, they'll probably receive a call asking whether they made a purchase in X country or Y state. The card companies have used this method for many years, and it's helped reduce some credit card fraud.

- **Experienced attorneys:** Although the resources I list here are usually quite helpful, you may want to contact an attorney to help you restore your credit and name if creditors aren't cooperative in removing fraudulent accounts from your credit report or charges from accounts. Contact the American Bar Association or Legal Aid office in your area and ask for the names of attorneys that specialize in the Fair Credit Reporting Act (FCRA), consumer law, and the Fair Credit Billing Act.

- **Your state's Attorney General's Office:** Check the website for your state's Attorney General's Office, which has resources about identity theft prevention.

Chapter 2

What's the Secret Password?

Some computers already allow you to access your information with fingerprints and other biometric scanners. However, those methods usually work for hardware only. If you want to get anything done on the Internet, you need passwords — many, many, many passwords. This chapter takes a look at all of those passwords (and security questions, as well) and what you can do to make them less hackable.

Hackable doesn't just refer to evil computer geniuses working their way into your computer to ferret out your most important data. The term also refers to far more common *social engineering,* in which people pair knowledge about you with other techniques to guess or obtain your passwords.

Choosing and Protecting Passwords

When you set up an e-mail account — or any account — on the Internet, you have to set a *password,* which is the keyword you type in to confirm your sign-in along with your user

ID. Passwords are not only used in e-mail, but also on almost every website you become a member of, and with many apps and devices. If you have a strong password, hackers will pass by your account and attempt to hack an easier target. In this section, I tell you how to make wise password choices and also how to protect those passwords after you've chosen them.

Picking a good password is not as thought-free — but *is* twice as important — as it may seem. Whoever has your password can (in effect) *be you* anywhere on the web — posting comments, sending spam e-mail messages, and leaving dangerous messages (which can range from pranks to scams or worse) for others to see. Basically, such an impostor can ruin your online reputation and possibly cause you serious financial grief.

So what goes into creating a fool-proof password? You could slam your hands into the keyboard and go with those results, but odds are you wouldn't remember what you entered. And you'd hurt your hands, but that's a different concern. Take a look at these more practical solutions:

- ✔ **Don't pick obvious passwords.** Don't use your first name or last name, or your dog's name, or your spouse's name, or your birthday, or your birthday backward, or common words in English, or any other common language. Someone who *really* wants to get access to your computer already knows to try this kind of personal information first. If you aren't feeling creative or otherwise up to the task of inventing random passwords, you can find free- ware and shareware password-generating applications by visiting CNET's Download.com and searching for *Password.*

- ✔ **Create longer passwords.** The longer the password, the better — 10,000 combinations are possible with a 4-digit password. The number of possible combinations for a 5-digit password is 100,000 (or 10x10x10x10x10). For a 6-digit password, the number is 1 million combinations.

- ✔ **Use both numbers *and* letters.** Throw a few letters into the password, and you really make things complicated. A 4-character password consisting of both letters and numbers has 1,679,616 possible combinations. (That's 10+26x10+26x10+26x10+26, for you math fans.) For a 5-character password, 60,466,176 combinations are possible.

✔ **Throw in a few symbols, like $, &, % and *, just to make guessing your password even harder.** The reason is obvious. Sometimes a software program or your operating system doesn't let you use nonalphanumeric characters, but if your system lets you, you certainly should! (This advice applies to your Internet Service Provider and other online passwords as well.)

A good password looks something like this: kl5K8$d.

Do the math, and you may suddenly feel very confident. After all, 10,000 possible combinations exist for a 4-digit password (for you math majors, that's 10x10x10x10 = 10,000). But, how long would it take a hacker to try all 10,000 of those combinations? With good password-cracking software — available for free from the web, of course — all it takes is about a minute.

The most common passwords: avoid, avoid, avoid!

You'd be surprised how many people use *password* or *passwd* as their login password. You can probably guess that these aren't strong passwords. These passwords are usually default passwords and need to be changed immediately. People use them because they're easy to remember. The following are the ten most commonly used passwords:

✔ password

✔ 123456

✔ 12345678

✔ Abc123

✔ qwerty

✔ monkey

✔ letmein

✔ dragon

✔ 111111

✔ baseball

Do *not* use any of these passwords. Most of the password-cracker programs have these passwords in them.

With any password, you should follow these common-sense rules to protect your privacy:

✔ Don't give your password to *anyone* — it's like giving away the keys to the front door of your house.

✔ If you even suspect that someone has your password, immediately change it.

✔ Change your password every few months just to be on the safe side. Maybe even rotate a group of passwords over the various accounts you use.

Storing and Remembering Your Passwords

I certainly can't remember all my passwords. Many websites ask you to enter a username and password. If you're buying an item from an online store such as Amazon.com, you create an account with a username and password that you enter every time you want to buy something. Amazon.com remembers your name, address, and credit card information as part of your account, so you don't need to enter it every time. If you want to read *The New York Times* online at www.nytimes.com, you create an account with a password, too. The account remembers what kinds of news you're interested in reading. After you use the web for a while, you pile up a heap of usernames and passwords. And widespread use of smartphones and tablets means that passwords are even more ubiquitous. Many apps require login, either for security or for data syncing. Even your device itself may require a PIN, password, or some kind of identifying action to gain access.

When a web page asks for a username and password, your browser may pop up a little window that offers to remember the username and password you enter, or the question may appear just above the top edge of the web page. If you click Yes, the next time you arrive at the same page, your browser may fill in your username and password for you.

Depending on who else has access to your computer, you might let your browser remember passwords to only those accounts that don't involve spending money or revealing personal information. For example, if I have an account at a

Harry Potter fan site that enables me to participate in online discussions, the danger of having someone break into this account is a lot less daunting than the thought of someone hacking into my online bank account. Unless your computer is in a physically secure place, don't let your browser remember passwords that have any real power.

As I mention earlier, the standard advice is to construct passwords from a mixture of letters, numbers, and symbols; to assign a different password to every account; to never write down passwords; and to change them every few months. Most people have dozens of accounts and ignore this advice because only a truly unusual person can remember dozens of different random passwords and which account goes with each one.

I suggest a compromise. Make up one good password to use on all your low-risk accounts — accounts in which letting someone else gain access has little consequence, such as online newspaper subscriptions. Use different passwords for the accounts that truly matter, such as online banking. Writing down these passwords and keeping them in a safe place is better than picking a password that's easy for someone to guess. Don't list your passwords in your desktop Rolodex or on a sticky note stuck to your computer's monitor.

You can use the password journal provided in this book — I won't tell anybody. Just make sure you update the passwords as you go and keep the book in a safe place. I'm talking secure, under-lock-and-key safe, not just "I left it in the car" safe. If you do write down any passwords, remember that you *and only you* should have access to that record.

You can also use password management programs like 1Password (https://agilebits.com/onepassword) or LastPass (https://lastpass.com/index.php?from website=1) to manage all of your browser-based passwords securely. These programs encrypt your passwords and restore them when needed, locking them away when not in use. Do your research and stick with the big names on this one. If you can't find any reviews or respected authorities talking about and endorsing the app, it isn't good enough for you. Word spreads quickly about bad software, so go with only the well-known quantities.

Understanding Password Vulnerabilities

Getting in to your home computer shouldn't require a blood test and a waiting period, but you can't let just anybody use your information, either. At this point, computer login services seem to have settled on requiring a *user ID* and a *secret password* which are usually adequate. However, passwords give a false sense of security. The bad guys know this and attempt to crack passwords as a step toward breaking into computer systems. Common words or combinations of characters just make it too easy. As much of a pain as it is, using a unique string of letters, characters, and numbers is better than a common term you can easily remember.

One big problem with relying solely on passwords for information security is that more than one person can know them. Sometimes, this is intentional; often, it's not. The tough part is that there's no way of knowing who, besides the password's owner, knows a password.

Knowing a password doesn't make someone an authorized user.

Even with good passwords, hackers can find some ways to get this information and access your systems. If your company doesn't make you choose a strong password or store that password correctly, whatever password you do use isn't all that secure. And now that more and more employees can work remotely, you don't always have the security of a private office.

Using Encryption

Encrypt a piece of data and suddenly it doesn't mean anything to anyone anymore — except for you and anyone else who has your password or key. Simply put, *encryption* scrambles data. So the fear of data being stolen or intercepted is gone because your data in the wrong hands is just gibberish.

If you use your encryption software to encrypt your list of passwords for safekeeping, you have to remember only one password: the one for your encryption software!

If the benefits of glorious gobbledygook sound good to you, here's how to put encryption to work on your own data:

- ✔ **Encrypt passwords.** Use a password encryption program, like RoboForm (www.roboform.com).

- ✔ **Encrypt files on your hard drive.** They're your files, darn it, and you don't want anyone else reading them. The trick, then, is to encrypt them so that if someone without the password does open your files, all he sees is something like this:

  ```
  dfjklsdfjkl;sdfjkl;fsdjkl;sdfjkl;sdfawe
  rtsdfjkl;sdfjkl;sdfajkl;dfgweruioerwjio
  or sdfjkl;werouiweruionjklsdflnjku90wer
  or xcvnm$9ke*sd893
  ```

  Lots of freeware and shareware programs are available that enable you to encrypt your files. To find them, browse to Download.com and search for *Encryption*.

Your computer operating system can also provide encryption options. Windows users should look up BitLocker (http://windows.microsoft.com/en-us/windows-8/bitlocker), and Mac users can rely on FileVault (http://support.apple.com/kb/HT4790).

Appreciating Password Enhancements

When you really want to keep your information secure, you can look into the following options to safeguard your passwords. The problem is that you can't really force accounts to use these measures. If a provider offers these features, then by all means take advantage of them! If the provider doesn't give you these options, you can still use a good password and keep your information as secure as possible. But you might encourage the provider to add these services as soon as possible (or look for a different provider).

- ✔ **Two-factor authentication:** This process may sound complicated, but two-factor authentication really helps keep your passwords private. Unfortunately, not all services require this feature. But Google does, so it's a good example. When you create a Google account, you can specify a mobile phone number to receive a text message when you try to log in to the account from an unfamiliar computer or device. Google sends a text message to the number with a code, and you must enter that code to access the account. An intruder is less likely to have your password and access to your phone, so your information remains safe. If a service offers two-factor authentication, use it!

✔ **Passphrases:** Just as hackers have to work a little harder to guess longer passwords, they have to work that much more with passphrases. You do have to spend a little more time typing "The quick brown fox jumps over the lazy dog" than you do "kZx43$," but you do keep your account far more secure.

Don't use "The quick brown fox jumps over the lazy dog" as a passphrase unless you want your account hacked by those persons who took typing classes in the mid- to late 20th century.

✔ **Captcha:** Never mind what captcha actually stands for — the effect is that you have to squint at a distorted picture of a series of characters and type those characters into a text field. This method prevents automated hacking attempts from gaining access to your account, presumably because only a human could discern what those characters actually are. Or they just frustrate us — one of the two.

✔ **VPN connection:** No matter what security method you use, it's always safer over a *virtual private network* (VPN). Most workplaces offer them, and you can buy commercial alternatives as well. These connections encrypt all traffic to and from your device, making it all the more safe for your use.

Answering Security Questions

Security questions have been around forever. Think of the cliché from war movies where a couple of GIs ask an approaching solider who won the World Series last year. On the Internet, these questions get a lot more personal, but the purpose is the same: to identify who you are in case a provider needs more verification (to reset a password, perhaps).

These security questions can range from your mother's maiden name to your favorite sports team or color. When you first create an account, you'll provide answers to the security questions, and the provider will ask for the answers when necessary. If the answers match, you're good. If not, you don't get access. Therefore, these questions tend to be rather precise (what was the name of your first pet?) rather than nebulous (how do you feel today?).

That said, *you don't have to answer correctly!* You just have to tell the service what you *told* it was the right answer the first time. You can give it a wrong answer when you set the question and remember to give it the wrong answer every time. For example, tell the service that your favorite team is the Cleveland Browns. Nobody ever guesses that.

Chapter 3

Viruses, Spyware, and Scams — Oh My!

*I*t doesn't matter how you do it; from the minute you connect your computer to the Internet, you've hung a giant neon welcome sign in front of your humble little cyber-abode.

Software companies have gotten better over the years when it comes to security, but they're still not perfect. Programs and operating systems still ship with security flaws. Why? Because security features cause operating systems to become complicated, and in the battle between high security and user friendliness, guess which one usually wins? Unfortunately, many of the holes are extremely difficult — if not impossible — for most users to find and turn off. On top of that, lots of popular Internet programs find their way into your device's information. It doesn't matter if it's a home computer or a mobile device — everything has some kind of hole in it.

Some of the scariest horror movies begin at home. Bad situations just seem a little more horrifying when they happen close to you. This chapter looks at some of the more common troubles you can encounter online and what you can do to avoid these terrors.

Investigating the Common Ways Your Information Can Be Compromised

As you read about viruses and all the other critters, you should remember that they're really just a means to an end.

So what's the end?

That depends on the goal of the program writer. Some critters are written to annoy; others are written to destroy. This distinction is particularly important to keep in mind because, even as you read this chapter, you can safely bet that someone, somewhere, is diligently working to find a new way to annoy or destroy that defies all the definitions in this section.

Viruses

A *virus* is a type of little program that loads onto your computer without your knowing it and then starts running amok. This section describes a few of the defining characteristics of a virus.

A virus can replicate itself and pass itself along to infect other computers — but only by burying itself inside something larger, such as a Microsoft Word document or the programming code of a piece of software, which then takes a ride to another computer on a disk, or as an e-mail attachment, or by some other method of file transfer.

In replicating themselves, viruses sometimes do their damage by making so many copies of themselves that they fill up your computer's memory and cause it to crash.

In many cases, the replication and spread of a virus are secondary to its primary function, which is to perform some other task (sometimes harmless, sometimes electronically fatal) inside your computer. For example, a more malicious virus may take complete control of your computer and order it to do something horrible like delete its own hard drive. Other viruses are intended as mere pranks: A good example is the Merry Christmas virus that simply flashes a harmless season's greeting on your screen in December — end of story. Or so you think, but now it's April Fools' Day and the Merry Christmas virus doesn't let you boot up your computer. Ha-ha-ha!

Worms

Forgive me for the analogy, but think *tapeworms* — the ones your mom always thought you had in your gut when you were a kid. Here's why the analogy is so fitting. *Worms* are similar to viruses in that they can copy themselves and do bad things to the computers they invade. Worms are also notorious loners, though, so they generally don't attach themselves to the programming code of files or dig deeply in the out-of-the-way corners of disks or hard drives, as viruses do. Instead, worms send copies of themselves over the Internet directly or they can hitch a ride in an e-mail message.

Macro viruses

A *macro virus* is a unique virus: Rather than be its own little program or application, it makes its appearance in the form of a *macro* embedded in a document file.

Some experts claim that nearly three-quarters of all viruses are macro viruses, in part because they can embed themselves in your software and attach themselves to every document you create, which allows them to spread easily to others.

To understand macro viruses, you first have to understand macros. Many software applications, including Word, Excel, and PowerPoint, allow you to create *macros,* which are nothing more than a way to record long series of commands and then repeat the series of commands over and over again with just a keystroke or two.

In some cases, macros add themselves to your default document template so that they're executed automatically every time you open an existing document or create a new one. That's how most macro viruses spread so quickly: Every time you create a new document in Word, the document is based on a default template named Normal.dotm that can contain font choices, margin settings, and, yes, even macros and macro viruses. If a macro virus is in your default template, you spread the virus every time you open or create a new document.

Trojan horses

A *Trojan horse* program tricks you into loading and running it by pretending to be something that it's not. (Surely you remember this story from Greek mythology.) The perfect example of a Trojan horse is a file that masquerades as an antivirus software patch but is really a virus.

Some Trojan horses are coupled with other types of viruses, such as macro viruses, which then generate new Trojan horses that are passed along to others.

Bots

After a malicious entity infects a computer, it can gather computers together to perform specific tasks, like spam several million e-mail accounts or try to take down a server. An infected computer is a *bot,* and many bots gather to form *botnets*. It's not bad enough that your computer is infected — botnets are like zombie armies gathered to perform hideous tasks (and probably gather more victims like themselves).

Spyware

Computer privacy experts define *spyware* as any piece of software that gathers information and uses your Internet connection to send that information somewhere else on your computer without your knowledge or approval. But why does the spyware do this? In many cases, the spyware is gathering information about you and your activities on your computer and sending that data back to the software manufacturer or some other data-collection company so that it can know more about you.

Protecting Yourself

Because I don't expect you to spend your life installing updates, here are some rules of thumb to figure out what updates you really need.

Get some antivirus software (like Norton or McAfee, or use a free version like AVG). Newer operating systems like Windows 8 can even have virus protection built in. And then remember to update your antivirus software consistently. The software is good, but without updated antivirus definitions that fight against current viruses (which are written and released almost every day), your antivirus software doesn't do you much good. Antivirus software manufacturers are continually updating these definitions, and you *must* get their updates from the web at least once a month — and every time you hear about a new virus that's storming the computer world like a plague.

The best way to make sure that your computer hasn't been hijacked is to run antivirus scans regularly. If your computer is connected to the Internet 24/7, you should also run a personal firewall program. A *personal firewall program,* among other safety features, helps you detect the presence of an intruder program by alerting you every time one of your programs — or, more importantly, a program being controlled by a hacker or zombie — tries to connect to services or locations on the Internet that you don't normally frequent.

More recent antivirus software packages automatically update their own definitions from the Internet so you don't have to. If you're absentminded, like me, you should invest in one of these auto-updating antivirus software programs even if an antivirus program is already installed on your computer.

Most antivirus software now blocks spyware as well, but you can also avoid it by not clicking unknown links or installing unknown software from the Internet. This includes that link that says your computer is already infected — it isn't now, but it will be after you click that link.

And don't forget to update your software, either! Privacy and security problems are most likely to show up in operating system, e-mail, and browser software, and other communications software, such as instant messenger programs. The good news is that the media is very good about covering stories about privacy holes in software — so you can be sure that if one of the programs you use has a problem, you'll hear about it. When you do, hightail it to the web and download the security fix. Operating systems and apps usually do a good job of letting you know when updates are ready, but don't be afraid to be proactive.

Mobile devices don't suffer as much vulnerability as PCs because they operate in a more closed environment and often use a locked operating system. However, just because it isn't a common occurrence doesn't mean it hasn't happened. Both major app stores (iOS and Android) have seen instances where potential malware found its way into downloadable apps. Both services were able to eliminate the threats remotely, but you still need to be aware of what you install on your device, and which links you click (even in SMS messages or apps like Twitter or Facebook). Consider anti-virus software for all of your devices, even your smartphone and tablet.

Recognizing Scams

Keep your eyes open and your head on a swivel and you'll avoid a lot of what the Internet has to throw at you. This section looks at common scams and how to avoid them.

Gone phishing

Eventually, you'll receive an e-mail that says it's from your bank, eBay, PayPal, or a similar website announcing a problem with your account. Invariably, the e-mail offers a handy link to click, saying that you must enter your username and password to set things in order.

Don't do it, no matter how realistic the e-mail and website may appear. You're seeing an ugly industry called *phishing.* Fraudsters send millions of these messages worldwide, hoping to convince a few frightened souls into typing their precious account name and password.

How do you tell the real e-mails from the fake ones? It's easy, actually, because *all* these e-mails are fake. Finance-related sites may send you legitimate history statements, receipts, or confirmation notices, but they will *never, ever* e-mail you a link for you to click and enter your password.

If you're suspicious, visit the company's *real* website by typing the web address by hand into Internet Explorer's Address bar. Chances are good that the real site won't list anything wrong with your account.

Many of the scams discussed in the following sections are types of phishing scams.

Card verification

Card verification scams are usually done by phone or via e-mail. The person calling or writing says that he needs to verify your credit card information for your account at some online merchant or pay service. He tells you that the server containing the credit card numbers has been hacked into and all the data on the credit card accounts has been lost, or he tells you that he's verifying your information to make sure that it's current. The caveat is that if you don't provide the information, he'll cancel your account.

If the scam is done by e-mail, the URL provided takes you to a site set up by the thieves, and when you enter the information to "verify" your credit card number, name, and expiration date, they capture the information on their server. Then — you know what happens — your card is used to make fraudulent charges. When the scam is done by phone, the thief writes down all the information needed to use your credit card for fraudulent purposes.

To avoid this scam, don't give the thieves the information either on the phone or online.

You won the lottery!

Here's how this scam works: You receive a letter, fax, or e-mail claiming that you've won a large sum of money in an overseas lottery game. You probably didn't know you even entered the lottery. The letter says that the lottery commission for whatever country's lotto has tried unsuccessfully to contact you about your windfall. To collect your winnings, you need to provide the lotto commission with your bank account information so that it can transfer the money to your account. Some of these scams have a form with the letter that asks for personal information such as your full name (including your middle name), birth date, address, occupation, marital status, and telephone number. Some of the forms also ask for next-of-kin information, including first and last name, address, telephone number, and occupation. What a great way to solicit more victims. The form also features a bank transfer section that asks for your bank's name, address, account numbers, routing number, and telephone number.

After you provide the information to the lotto commission, the only one who wins is the person who sent the letter. Imagine that! To avoid becoming a victim, don't give out this information. Just discard the letter, e-mail, or fax.

These lottery scams have been successful because they play to the greed aspect of human nature. There's no such thing as free money.

Bogus charities

You're watching TV, and the phone rings. You answer, and the person on the other end says that she's from a charitable group soliciting donations. Be careful. This has been used as a ploy to get your credit card number and expiration date, or a personal check.

Legitimate charities use telephone solicitation for donations, but you can give to your favorite charity and still protect yourself. Many charities offer alternatives to making a donation over the phone. For instance, go online and look up the charity. The website will have all the contact information to make a donation.

Another variation on this theme is the disaster relief donation scam. An example of this scam occurred right after the September 11 tragedy. The thieves set up a bogus website and then sent a spam e-mail soliciting $25 credit card donations to help the victims' families. The e-mail had a link to the thief's website, and the recipient clicked the link to enter the site to make a donation. The site asked, of course, for your credit card number and expiration date as well as your full name. Also, the site asked for your SSN under the guise that you can then claim the donation on your income tax as a deduction.

People who made the donation found themselves victims of identity theft. The perpetrators established new addresses and opened new accounts, using the names of the people who went to the site.

Other people were pressured into making on-the-spot donations over the phone, using the same tactics that the website
thieves used to get personal information.

Don't stop donating to charities — just don't give out your
personal information to strangers on the telephone. In most
states, the charitable organizations must be registered with
the state Attorney General, so check whether the charity is
legitimate before you donate.

Bogus invoices

This scam involves phony invoices made to look like the real
thing. I've been getting a number of these bogus invoices in my
e-mail recently. This may be the new trend to garner personal
information from you. I've also received some bogus invoices
via U.S. mail. One of the telltale signs of a bogus invoice is the
lack of a phone number for an alternative contact method.

To comply with U.S. Postal Service regulations, solicitations
are required to have the following wording. The following
disclaimer is easy to spot in the postal mail, but I haven't
always seen the disclaimer in e-mail messages.

> **THIS IS NOT A BILL. THIS IS A SOLICITATION. YOU
> ARE UNDER NO OBLIGATION TO PAY THE AMOUNT
> STATED ABOVE UNLESS YOU ACCEPT THIS OFFER.**

The wording is required to be near the top of the invoice in
capital letters, in bold type, and at least as large as the letters
on the solicitation. Often the disclaimer is overlooked or mis-
understood. The idea is to get you to pay for something you
didn't order. Sometimes the scam is used to solicit credit card
information.

Don't respond to invoices that don't have phone numbers on
them. If you didn't order what's stated in the invoice, simply
ignore it.

Phony brokerage firms

In the phony brokerage-firm scam, the thieves set up a website using the name of an actual brokerage firm, but they
use a different address. Then they craft and send a spam

e-mail. The e-mail usually trumpets upcoming "hot" stock to entice you into visiting its website. On the site, you provide your credit card number and other personal information to purchase the "stock." At the time of this writing, it isn't clear whether the scam is being perpetrated to garner personal information to use in further identity theft frauds or whether it's collecting money for phony stocks.

In any event, don't purchase stocks from unsolicited e-mails; it's probably just a ruse to get your personal information, or it's not a good tip anyway. If you're interested in buying stock, contact one of the brokerage firms near you and set up a face-to-face meeting in its office.

Temporary suspension of your account

The scam touting a temporary suspension of your account is set up either in an e-mail or a telephone call. The thieves use the scare tactic that your bank account (or online payment or online auction account) has been suspended. The e-mail sender or phone caller claims that the bank is reviewing all of its accounts to eliminate waste and fraud. You're then requested to visit the "company's" website to provide the information necessary to do a review of your account and to make sure that the information on file is correct. The information they ask for is the usual: full name, account number, ATM or debit card number, and PIN. The e-mail sender or phone caller goes on to say that if you don't provide the information, your account will be permanently canceled.

You know what happens next! You become the victim of identity theft. Don't provide the information. Contact your bank instead.

Job scams

Several times per week, you probably receive e-mail invitations to work at home or as a shipping clerk or to transfer funds for various companies. These are usually scams. If you fall for them, you could lose money and put your personal information — such as your address, SSN, bank account number, and so on — into the wrong hands. Don't apply for unsolicited job offers even if the e-mail states that your information was garnered from a job website.

Most of these bogus job scams suck you in with the promise of thousands of dollars for working a few hours a day from your home. Some of the job scams can land you in trouble with the law because the activities you're asked to perform involve money laundering and repackaging of merchandise bought with stolen credit cards.

You can find out whether an e-mail job offer is a scam by going to www.scambusters.org. That website describes numerous scams, and you can search by the type of scam.

Chapter 4

Shop 'til You Drop — Securely

*T*he greatest gift the Internet gave to us, of course, is ani-
mated GIFs. The second greatest gift might be the ability
to locate and purchase just about anything in the world you
might want. Point, click, type in a few numbers, and you're
ready to go! That said, you have to be sure exactly who is
taking your money and whether that person will actually send
you what you're expecting (such as a real iPad instead of just
the box that once contained an iPad). This chapter helps you
identify authentic websites and ensure that your financial
transactions are conducted with the highest possible security.

Taking a Close Look at Websites

Look around and be choosy. If you walk into a restaurant
and see a dirty floor and signs of mice or you're assaulted
by an unpleasant odor, I hope you would turn around and
walk out. If you're smart, you apply the same principle when
shopping and banking on the web. Look around before you
whip out your credit card. Ask yourself, "Does this site look
like somebody put it up over a weekend? Or does it look like
someone worked really hard to make my shopping experience a positive one? Has the company successfully instilled
in me a sense of confidence and trust?" If not, it's time to go
shopping someplace else.

Just as you can't judge a book by its cover, the legitimacy of a website is hard to gauge just by looking. If you see signs of poor quality, you may want to consider moving along.

If it sounds too good to be true. . . you already know what I'm going to say.

Use the power of the Internet to investigate. Just because you've never heard of a website doesn't mean that it isn't a good company. Look up reviews on Google or check social media. Chances are, if something went wrong, people are talking about it.

Your bank's website: How safe is it?

You have money. You keep it someplace other than under your mattress: in a bank, a credit union, or a savings and loan. When you want access to your cash, you may get it in a variety of ways. The old-fashioned way, which includes a trip to the bank, is always an option, or you can write a check. Or, you may want to access your money electronically, which you can do with your debit card or by using the web.

Online banking may still have a few issues here and there, but for the most part, you can interact with your financial institutions online with no problem. These institutions have taken great pains to ensure the safety of your (and their) money, but think of it as, well, a physical bank. The bank is as safe as the company can make it, but you still have to take the proper precautions (security guards, proper procedures, and the like). The good news is that you can do lots of things today to make sure that your online banking transactions are as safe as possible:

> ✔ **Tales from the (en)Crypt:** Make sure that both your browser and your bank's website use 128-bit encryption, which, by some estimates, is so safe that it would take more than a trillion years for a hacker to crack using current technologies.
>
> How will you know if your browser offers 128-bit encryption? Most browsers tell you. For example, Microsoft Internet Explorer has an About Internet Explorer option on the Help menu. Choose that option to see what version

of the browser you're using, and in most cases it includes *Cipher strength,* indicating the number of bits used for encryption.

✔ **Look for a secure server:** This advice goes hand in hand with ensuring 128-bit encryption, but the secure server gives you a visual clue that it's working. Look for the locked padlock icon on your browser and the addition of the letter *s* to the *http* — as in *https* — at the beginning of your bank's URL.

✔ **Get some insurance:** Is this bank insured by the Federal Deposit Insurance Corporation (FDIC)? To be sure, check out the FDIC website at FDIC.gov:

```
http://research.fdic.gov/bankfind
```

✔ **Get it in writing, Part I:** Check your bank's website for a written guarantee that protects you from losses from fraud that may result from online banking.

✔ **Get it in writing, Part II:** Hey, you never know when trouble may occur. You'll get into much less trouble, though, if you have printed copies of all your online transactions to prove that what you say is true.

Evaluating an online shop

Here are some questions to keep in mind when you're shopping online. Astute shoppers will notice that these questions are the same ones to keep in mind wherever you're shopping:

✔ Can you find the appropriate digital certificates and the VeriSign logo that indicate the website is authentic?

✔ Do you regularly receive e-mail confirmation of your purchases?

✔ Does the website provide a clear and complete privacy policy?

✔ Are the descriptions clear enough to know what you're ordering?

✔ Are the prices competitive, with other online stores *and* with mail-order and regular retail?

✔ Does the store have the products in stock, or does it offer a firm shipping date?

✔ Does the store have a good reputation?

✔ Does the store have a clearly written privacy policy that limits what it can do with the data it collects from you?

✔ Can you ask questions about your order?

✔ How can you return unsatisfactory goods?

Guard Your Card While Shopping Online

Shopping the web is probably not as dangerous as trying to find a parking space at the mall 45 minutes before closing time on Christmas Eve. You could wear a hard hat and safety boots. You could attach a seat belt to your desk chair. Or you could simply follow these common-sense rules.

Ordering stuff without sharing your primary account information

Purchasing merchandise online is incredibly easy, but you must protect yourself. Here are some alternatives to using your own bank account or card on a shopping site:

✔ **Use a one-time-use credit card number for online purchases.** This comes from your bank, has a different number than your actual account number, and is good for the single transaction. This prevents you from exposing your credit card number online or through malware you may not know exists on your computer.

✔ **Use a stored value card.** This is like a prepaid phone card. You purchase the card with a certain dollar amount and each time you use it, the purchase amount is subtracted from the balance. For example, you could buy an iTunes card and use it for your iTunes purchases, or you could buy a Visa prepaid card and use it for everything else.

✔ **Use an online payment service.** Through this service, you can set up an account and make purchases drawing from that account. For example, PayPal is one of the most popular and trusted online payment services.

Embracing safe shopping practices

Follow these guidelines to protect your accounts when you're shopping online:

- ✔ **Use the latest Internet browser.** The browser allows you to navigate the Internet and provides *encryption,* which scrambles data sent to a server to protect it. When you use the most recent browser version, you're also using the latest encryption version.

- ✔ **Use only one credit card (or a debit card that's not attached to your primary savings or checking account) to make purchases on the Internet.** This way, you can track your purchases and activity on the card more easily. This is a good way to keep a record of all your Internet transactions to help ensure accuracy of your card's charges. If the card is compromised, you can cancel it and get a new one. These days, online sites request the security code to complete the transaction, just as it is for phone orders. Merchants ask for the security code to help protect them from fraudulent charges, and the code also helps protect you because the identity thief has to get the code to complete the transaction.

- ✔ **Don't give your password or ID online unless you know who you're dealing with, even if your Internet service provider (ISP) asks for it via e-mail.** This request is a scam and is used by identity thieves to collect personal information.

- ✔ **Don't store your credit card online with a service.** It's awfully convenient to store a credit card or two on Amazon or iTunes to facilitate quick purchasing. And the services *want* you to do it — that's why they make it so easy! Just click the button and it's yours! But that means that anybody with access to your account can just as easily get the information (and get the product shipped to them, of course). If you're really concerned about keeping this information safe, refuse to let these services store any credit card information. This policy makes online shopping a little more inconvenient, and you'll have to type in that information *every single time*, but the added security and peace of mind could be worth it to you.

This advice can be a lifesaver if you have children in the house. If you don't store a credit card, you don't have to worry about games with in-app purchases racking up huge bills on your credit card.

✔ **Never include any sensitive information in an e-mail message.** Websites go to great lengths to secure information entered into their web forms. That security won't make it to e-mail messages. You should never write out a credit card number and three-digit security code in an e-mail message and then send it to somebody. That action means that both you and the recipient have a copy of the e-mail with this information, and you're twice as likely to see that information be hacked. Furthermore, somebody could possibly intercept that e-mail (not common, but it has happened) and get your information that way. Sending sensitive information via e-mail is never a good idea. Use a secure web form instead.

By the way, that suggestion to never send information in an e-mail applies to Social Security numbers, bank account numbers, passwords, or just about anything else except for happy cat photos. Everybody loves happy cat photos.

Chapter 5

Staying Safe on Social Media

- -

In This Chapter

▶ Knowing how to network safely

▶ Staying safe on Facebook, Twitter, and YouTube

- -

*M*ore than likely, you have at least one social media account. Perhaps you're interacting with social media right now. (Tell your daughter that the baby pictures are wonderful and you can't wait to see her family at Thanksgiving.) But these accounts provide a lot of information to the outside world, and that information can be used to hack your passwords and personal accounts. This chapter shows you how to avoid those problems, allowing you to focus on the baby pictures and holiday plans with a clear head.

Networking Online

Nowadays people often meet and talk with their friends and share experiences on online networking sites, such as Facebook and Twitter. You need to be careful about how much personal information you post online. The more you post, the easier you make it for the thief posing as a friend to get your information and steal your identity.

Knowing what information to keep private

The best advice I can give you is to keep your personal information offline. Of course, you wouldn't put your Social Security Number (SSN) online, but what about

- ✔ Your date of birth?
- ✔ The city where you live?
- ✔ Your cellphone number?
- ✔ Your name? A pseudonym?

Do you give that information to those who have befriended you on a private chat page? Personal networking pages aren't the only pages where you need to be careful with sharing personal information; the same logic applies to professional networking pages. You can post a resumé, but you don't need to include any personal information, such as your home address. Prospective employers can contact you initially by e-mail.

Use the same discretion online that you would when meeting friends in public, new or old. Don't share your SSN, your birth date (not right away, anyway), your full name, and so on. Be wary of someone who asks too many personal questions while networking. If you feel uncomfortable, it's probably for a good reason. Listen to your intuition; these feelings are often correct.

Following some guidelines

Here are some simple rules to follow when networking online:

- ✔ **Do not post personal information on public pages.** Things to exclude are
  - *Date of birth (DOB)*
  - *SSN*
  - *Address* (including the city where you live)
- ✔ **Strongly consider excluding the following from your public pages.**
  - *Full name:* Some social networks do require you to use your REAL name, but you don't have to tell

them everything. Leave out your middle name and other identifiers, like Jr., Sr., or numbers.

- *Pictures of yourself:* This can be a sticky subject, especially regarding LinkedIn or sites with other professional functions. If you must post a picture that can be viewed by everybody on the Internet, ensure that the account contains only information tied to your business. Everything else should be left out.

✔ **Be careful who you allow to see your personal pages.**

- This is true especially for those whom you meet online because people who use the Internet to prey on other people are out there.

- Keep your circle of contacts on your personal page to those who you know in real life and not just from the Internet (but still be careful).

✔ **Be skeptical of anyone you just met (especially online) who attempts to get too close.**

- If this person claims to be a friend of one of your friends, verify it.

- If this person asks too many questions that make you feel uncomfortable, do not give them any information.

✔ **Avoid answering questions about schools you attended, what year you graduated, or even your pet's name.** Answers to these questions can help someone figure out your year of birth or the answer to security questions you choose in case you forget your password(s).

✔ **Avoid making family connections on social networking sites.** Doing so provides too much information — such as your mother's maiden name, your place of birth, and so on — that potential identity thieves can use to get other information about you.

Setting Boundaries

Social media allows you to make connections all over the world with people you would never meet otherwise, and it helps you keep in touch with the ones you love. But all of that personal information can make it easier to access your accounts. Above all, keep this one directive in mind:

If somebody doesn't need to know something, don't tell them that something.

Consider the following guidelines when you're using some of the most popular social media sites.

Facebook

No one wants anything bad to happen to you as a result of something you do on Facebook. You don't want that. Facebook doesn't want that. I definitely don't want that. I hope that these explanations help to prevent anything bad from happening to you on Facebook. But no matter what, *you* need to take part in keeping yourself safe. To ensure your own safety on Facebook, you have to make an effort to be smart and safe online.

So what *is* your part? Your part is to be aware of what you're putting online and on Facebook by asking yourself a few questions:

- ✔ Is what I'm putting on Facebook legal?
- ✔ Would I be embarrassed by someone in particular finding this information?
- ✔ Will the audience with whom I'm sharing this information use it in a way I trust?

You need to be the one to choose whether displaying any given piece of information on Facebook is risky. If it's risky, you need to be the one to figure out the correct privacy settings for showing this information to the people you choose to see it — and not to the people you don't.

You should also make good use of features like Facebook Friends lists. These lists allow you to determine a subgroup of your friends that you can share specific information with — information that doesn't go out to the rest of your friends. Use a Close Friends list to post more personal stuff, and share your fabulous vacation photos with everybody you wish to bore or make jealous.

Facebook Friends lists work only when you address your posts to the correct list. If you share the wrong thing with the wrong people, you've circumvented your own security policy. Check the list *before* you post!

 Your part is equivalent to the part you play in your everyday life to keep yourself safe: You know which alleys not to walk down at night, when to buckle your seat belt, when to lock the front door, and when to toss the moldy bread before making a sandwich. Add these to your list:

   ✔ I use my Facebook privacy settings wisely.

   ✔ I am careful about what information I expose to lots of people.

Twitter

Above all else, remember that Twitter is a public forum. Even when you're talking to your trusted Twitter network, your tweets are very much public; Google and other search engines index them, and anyone on the web can link to them.

 Protect your account by adjusting your settings to prevent search engines and the occasional passerby from viewing your updates.

All the public exposure that Twitter offers can really help promote you and your business, but that exposure also comes with some responsibilities:

   ✔ **Use common sense!** Don't publicly tweet or @reply someone your address, phone number, or other personal details that you should keep private. Send that kind of information via DM (direct message) — or, even better, via e-mail, instant message, or phone call. Keeping your personal details private protects both you and anyone in your care, such as your kids.

   ✔ **Use DMs cautiously.** Typing **d or dm** *username* and then your message does send a private direct message from any Twitter interface. But trust us, if you make a typo *e*, you would not be the first person to accidentally post a private DM publicly. Ensure you use the correct syntax for a DM (or better yet, use the direct message functionality embedded in whatever client you use to access Twitter).

To avoid accidental updates, make it a habit to use the Message button on a user's page, double-check your **d *username*** tweets before posting, or use `http://twitter.com/direct_messages` to send DMs. You want to be extremely careful if you decide to send sensitive information by DM. Better yet, use an even more secure medium like e-mail or even encryption. *Never* send passwords, credit card numbers, Social Security numbers, or other valuable private data by Twitter (or even e-mail, for data that sensitive).

✔ **Maintain boundaries.** Try to be aware of how you are (or aren't) maintaining boundaries with the people you interact with frequently on Twitter. Especially before you agree to meet someone in person, take a look at how you've interacted in the past and make sure that you've kept your relationship clear from the start, whether it's for business or friendship.

YouTube

You are your username. For most of the YouTube community, that's all you are. Registering with YouTube is an anonymous procedure — you don't need to give your name, just your e-mail address. YouTube keeps that information private, so really, all that other YouTube users know about you automatically is your username. Any other information is divulged by you.

Keep your identity a secret. Let them call you Batman, not Bruce Wayne. YouTube is a community of millions of people, and you seldom truly know who it is you're interacting with. That's why the best policy — the smartest policy — is to use the Tube within the shelter of your anonymous username.

The following is a list of things to consider when using YouTube anonymously:

✔ **Don't use your full name as your username.** Be johniscool rather than johnsmith. That might seem obvious, but it's not always the case. That's because many people use YouTube for exactly that reason: to get their names out there. If you're a comedian, chances are that you want your name on your videos. You want an agent.

You want to get hired. It only makes sense. If you're not trying to get famous on YouTube, though, don't post your full name anywhere.

✔ **Don't reveal too much in your videos.** If, for some reason, your video contains footage of the outside of your house, avoid showing your full address. In other words, if I see the number 24 on the door and then in a later frame see you and your husband walking the dog past a street sign that reads *Princeton*, I have a pretty good idea of where you live. For the same reason, avoid showing the license plate on your car.

✔ **Be careful with kids and the family videos.** One of the greatest things about YouTube is that you can easily share videos with family and friends across the miles. For family videos, upload them as *private videos* — ones that can be viewed only by people you designate.

✔ **Don't reveal too much on your channel.** Customizing your channel on YouTube is a great way to introduce yourself to the YouTube community, creating a place where users can go to see all the videos that you upload and to learn more about you. However, make sure that they don't learn too much. Unless you're looking to get famous or want to be contacted by any random person on the Tube, don't post your full name or personal contact information. Remember that your channel is no more private than any other page on YouTube.

✔ **Think twice before giving out your personal e-mail address.** People often forget that YouTube is a chat site as well as a video-sharing site. You can message other users, and they can message you. But stay clear on this point: Any messages you send or receive are sent *through* YouTube. In other words, if someone watches one of your videos and sends you a message, he sent that message to your username. That's anonymous. He does not have your real e-mail address. You can swap messages anonymously — using just your username — with any other Tuber, so there's no real need for you to give your personal e-mail address to any other user.

✔ **Consider carefully what you write in messages, comments, or feedback.** You probably aren't planning on getting into fights with people on the Tube, but you might be surprised at how easily things can get heated.

Some Tubers leave nasty comments, and you might be tempted to fire off a response. That's not a violation, but don't get so angry that you arrange a meeting place for a real-life fight. That might sound crazy, but believe it or not, it happens.

On the flip side, you might not be planning on falling in love on the Tube either, but you just might find yourself involved in a message exchange with some charming Tuber out there. Believe it or not, this happens, too. And what a coincidence — he lives in your city! He's rich, he's a brain surgeon, he looks like George Clooney, and he wants to meet you for a drink. Should you go? That's entirely up to you, but don't forget that this is a *total* stranger, and he just might not *really* be that handsome devil you see in his videos. Whatever you do, do not message that person your personal info. If you go out on a limb and actually meet that person — this is not something that I advise you to do, by the way — and sparks don't fly, you probably won't want him to know how to get back in touch.

✔ **Don't tell anybody your password.** YouTube will *never* ask you to reveal your password for any reason. If you get a message from YouTube asking for your password, that message is not really from YouTube. You're being scammed by someone, somehow, some way.

✔ **Don't be guilty of libel.** *Libel* is defamation by written or printed words, pictures, or in any form other than by spoken words. What this means for you on YouTube is that you should be careful of making accusations or allegations about other Tubers. Don't say that someone is a thief. Don't say that someone has a disease, that he's insane, that he's a murderer, or that he's cheating on his spouse. Will you get sued? It might not be likely, but it's not impossible.

✔ **Don't assume that YouTube knows who every user is.** When someone registers with YouTube, all that she supplies is an e-mail address. No name. No credit card. So don't make the mistake in thinking that YouTube has the 411 on every user or that every user can ultimately be held accountable for his or her behavior.

Chapter 6

Ten Things You Should Never Do with Your Password

*E*verybody's password (or PIN or passphrase or whatever you use) is different, or else there wouldn't be any reason to use them. That said, there are some common pitfalls that anybody with passwords should avoid, and this chapter lists the most common (and the most troublesome). Keep these scenarios in mind as you navigate the Internet, and don't let yourself be an easy target!

Write Your Password on Your Keyboard

Anybody walking by your computer could get access at a glance if you write down your password on or under your keyboard. Step away for a quick second for some coffee, and that's all it takes. That's also all it takes for somebody to steal the computer altogether, but why make it easier for your thieves by giving them the password as well?

Use the Same Password over Multiple Sites

After a thief has access to your e-mail password, for example, that same password could get them access to a whole host of other sites, most of which are probably identified by the messages those sites send to your e-mail account. Using separate passwords for each site (or at least your most important sites, like banking and credit card accounts) helps maintain a better level of security for your information.

E-Mail Somebody Your Password

If you do decide to share a password with someone you trust, don't share it via e-mail. Not only does Netflix get really angry when you share your account, but you don't know what could happen to the e-mail account of the person to whom you send the e-mail. Just because you do your best to ensure security on your accounts doesn't mean everybody does.

Share Your Password With Somebody You Don't Know

If you wouldn't trust someone with your wallet or your car, don't trust her with your password. There's no telling who's on the other side of that e-mail account or phone number. Ask anybody who's ever exchanged pleasantries over e-mail with a Nigerian prince asking for a little financial transaction.

Use Common Words in Your Password

Sure, ordinary words may be easy for you to remember, but they're easy for everybody to guess as well. Thieves know them, and the tools they use to break into accounts try these words before anything else. Avoid using words in passwords entirely!

You should also avoid using common sequences of numbers, as well. Any variation on "!23456" is just too easy to guess. You could try to use all of the digits in pi, but that's just too easy to guess as well. Who doesn't know all of the digits in pi by heart?

Really?

Okay, but that's still too many numbers to type out. Use something else.

Use Your Birth Date in Your Password

Via social media or other resources, it's easy for others to find out your date of birth. Again, why make theft easier? Avoid including any number that can easily be linked to you in your password. And don't use your anniversary date, either — you'll never remember it.

Use Any Identifying Number as Your Password

Any number that people can easily associate with you doesn't belong in your password. Phone numbers are too easy to link to your account, and leaving your Social Security number in a database (even a supposedly secure password database) is just too dangerous. Keep your personal numbers out of your password.

Use Your Child's Name in Your Password

Don't include your child's name in any password you create. This advice applies to any family member, really, but especially to children. Especially if you're one of those people who uses your child's photo as your Facebook profile photo. How easy is it for a thief to make that connection?

Note that, in this case, pets are most definitely considered family members. They are certainly worth a place in your heart, but not in your password.

Type Your Password on a Device You Don't Trust

You've probably developed a level of comfort with your home PC or smartphone. Your electronic devices are around you all the time, you've gotten to know them, and you can personally ensure that they're safe because you're the only one who uses them.

Unless your kids use them — I don't know if you can trust them or not.

Still, you can pretty much guarantee the safety of your personal devices. You can't guarantee that same level of safety at a computer offered at a hotel business center or a library or any other common computer. A good rule is that if you don't have permissions to install software on the computer, you probably shouldn't be typing important passwords on that computer, either.

Type Your Password When Using the Internet on a Network You Don't Trust

Hey, look! That network advertised on the sign that says FREE WIFI at the airport or hotel surely has to be safe, right?

Please, stop right there.

If you've never been on the network before and it seems too good to be true, please stay off of that network. Verify that any public network you're on is valid before conducting important business on it. If you're at a hotel or airport or even somebody else's house, ask someone with some authority or knowledge before you access the network. And even then, use a VPN to ensure that your traffic is secure and encrypted before you proceed with any major decisions, like taking out a mortgage or Tweeting a picture of your meal.

Some things are just too important to risk.

Part II
Passwords & Internet Addresses Journal

Create an Account

Email: [   ]

Password: [   ]

Retype password: [   ]

Security question: [Choose a question ▼]

What is your name?

What is your quest?

What is the airspeed velocity of an unladen swallow?

Create a question

Answer: [   ]

(Continue)

In this part . . .

*F*ollowing the rules of safe password creation — creating complex passwords that aren't dictionary words, using a combination of letters and numbers, changing your passwords regularly, and assigning a different password for each account — can make remembering those passwords really difficult. In this directory, you can record your usernames, passwords, and security questions and answers so that you can log into your accounts whenever you want without taking the time to coax your memory into revealing the magic words. Just remember one thing: Keep this book in a safe place!

Chapter 7

Creating an Inventory of All Your Accounts

*I*n a perfect world, you wouldn't need to write down your passwords to remember them. You might not even need passwords in a perfect world. And the ice cream would be free, too. We don't live in that world, though, so this chapter gives you a place to record passwords to reference when your memory fails you.

Leaving your computer, electronic devices, and this book, out and available to the public is never safe. Keep these items safe and secure!

To help you get started filling in the journal pages that follow, here's a list of typical password-protected accounts that most of us have to set up as we do our electronic banking, shopping, playing, and other activities. Use the list as a reminder for the various passwords you might have created and then jot them down in the appropriate place in this journal.

Just like a good old-fashioned address book, you'll find alphabetized thumb tabs along the outside of the pages to help you find your passwords later. So be sure to put your Facebook password in the Fs, your Google password in the Gs, and so forth. You'll also find space to make updates whenever you change your password.

Communications

If you've used the Internet for a while, you likely have an e-mail password. As you get more accustomed to the online world, you might create a blog or file-sharing account as well. Remember that the passwords for such sites access not only your ability to use these accounts, but also the content you keep in these accounts. Use unique passwords for each of these accounts!

- Blogs (including WordPress and Blogger)
- E-mail (if you use Google, Yahoo!, or Microsoft, this password will be the same as those accounts)
- Skype
- Online forums
- File-sharing sites (including Dropbox and Google Drive)

Share only those files that you have the rights and permissions to share. Services like BitTorrent provide a valuable service to disseminate software quickly and efficiently, and you shouldn't use those services to illegally share music, movies, and the like.

Entertainment

Entertainment sites hold the keys to your online fun, including video- and music-streaming services. These passwords don't *usually* include financial information, but you should still never share these passwords with anybody else. Who knows how somebody's viewing habits will mess up your Netflix recommendations?

- ✔ Amazon Prime (this password will be the same as your Amazon password)
- ✔ Dailymotion
- ✔ Hulu
- ✔ Image-sharing sites (including Imgur, Instagram, and Flickr)
- ✔ Fantasy sports
- ✔ Netflix
- ✔ Newspaper and news sites
- ✔ Pandora
- ✔ Online gaming sites (including Xbox and Steam)
- ✔ Casino rewards programs
- ✔ Spotify
- ✔ Magazine subscriptions
- ✔ YouTube (this password will be the same as your Google password)
- ✔ Movie rentals (including Blockbuster and Redbox)
- ✔ Restaurant reservation services (including OpenTable)
- ✔ Recipe sites
- ✔ Phone apps

Financial

The passwords you create for sensitive financial information, including bank accounts, credit cards, and loans, are some of your most important passwords. You should *never* repeat a password across multiple financial accounts. Make every password unique!

- ✔ 401k
- ✔ IRA and other retirement accounts
- ✔ Credit cards

✔ Bank accounts

✔ Investment accounts

✔ Mortgage

✔ Credit score–reporting services

✔ ATM PIN

✔ Financial-planning software (including Quicken or Mint)

✔ Tax preparation software

✔ Payroll and paycheck services

✔ Auto, student, or other loans

Hardware

Gadgets and hardware often require passwords to access user screens or applications. As long as you don't let anybody else use these devices, you're probably pretty safe with these passwords. But still, make sure you don't leave these passwords lying around near the gadgets in question — just to be safe.

✔ iPad or other tablet

✔ iPhone or other smartphone

✔ PC

✔ Laptop

✔ Home Wi-Fi network

✔ Home router

✔ Home modem

Search and Information Sites

Search engine sites have grown from places where you look for things online to expansive sites that offer e-mail, networking, and other services. Note that a single password can access several different services, so I've tried to identify as many of them as possible.

- AOL (includes e-mail and other services)
- Ask.com
- Google (includes Gmail, YouTube, Google+, Google Drive, and a whole host of other services)
- Microsoft (includes Bing, Outlook.com, SkyDrive, and other options including Xbox content)
- Yahoo! (includes e-mail and additional information services)
- IMDb (Internet Movie Database)
- Weather sites

Shopping

Most online retailers require you to set up an account with a password before making a purchase. Remember that many of these services can store financial and payment information depending on your preferences, so guard these passwords as much as you would your credit card or bank account numbers.

- Amazon
- iTunes (includes music, videos, and apps — usually the same as your Apple ID)
- eBay
- Etsy
- PayPal
- Department stores (including Target or Walmart)
- Online discount sites (including Groupon and Woot)
- Craigslist
- Travel (including Travelocity, Expedia, and Orbitz)
- Tickets (including Ticketmaster and StubHub)
- Rewards programs (including Starbucks and Walgreens)

Social

If you use a computer and go online regularly, you probably have a social media account or two (or twelve). Because these accounts are often the targets of hacking or phishing attempts, change these passwords frequently and use unique passwords for each account.

- ✔ Facebook
- ✔ Twitter
- ✔ Myspace
- ✔ reddit
- ✔ Dating sites (including eHarmony, Match.com, and OkCupid)
- ✔ Tumblr
- ✔ Yelp
- ✔ TripAdvisor
- ✔ Pinterest

Utilities and Services

This section includes passwords associated with the bills you pay every month, week, or year. As much as you're hoping somebody else will pay them for you, use a unique password for each of these accounts. These accounts often store sensitive information like bank account numbers or other personally identifiable information. The better sites store this information securely, but why take the risk?

- ✔ Monthly Utilities
  - Electricity
  - Water
  - Sewer

- Gas
- Heating
- Trash services
- Recycling services
- Home phone (landline)
- Mobile phone
- Internet service provider

✔ Cable or satellite television

✔ Satellite radio

✔ Medical (including care providers, facilities, and pharmacies)

✔ Insurance (including health, auto, and home)

✔ Reimbursement savings accounts

✔ Bureau or Department of Motor Vehicles

✔ Other bill-paying accounts

Work and School

This section includes passwords you use while at work or while studying. Be sure that you adhere to any applicable school or work security policies when creating and possibly writing down these passwords. I don't want to get you in any trouble!

✔ LinkedIn

✔ Work network credentials

✔ Work e-mail account (if different than personal e-mail account)

✔ School network credentials

✔ School e-mail account (if different than personal or work e-mail account)

- ✔ School network accounts for your children
- ✔ Online courses
- ✔ Antivirus or security accounts
- ✔ Voice mail
- ✔ Tech support services

Site name: _____

Web address: _____

A–B

Username: _____

Password	Date

Site notes:

A–B

Site name: _____

Web address: _____

Username: _____

Password	Date

Site notes:

Site name: _____

Web address: _____

A–B

Username: _____

Password	Date

Site notes:

A–B

Site name: _____

Web address: _____

Username: _____

Password	Date

Site notes:

Site name: _____

Web address: _____

Username: _____

A–B

Password	Date

Site notes:

A–B

Site name: _____

Web address: _____

Username: _____

Password	Date

Site notes:

Site name: _____

Web address: _____

Username: _____

A–B

Password	Date

Site notes:

A–B

Site name: _____

Web address: _____

Username: _____

Password	Date

Site notes:

Site name: _____

Web address: _____

Username: _____

C–D

Password	Date

Site notes:

Site name: _____

Web address: _____

Username: _____

C–D

Password	Date

Site notes:

Site name: _____

Web address: _____

Username: _____

C–D

Password	Date

Site notes:

Site name: _____

Web address: _____

Username: _____

C–D

Password	Date

Site notes:

Site name: _____

Web address: _____

Username: _____

C–D

Password	Date

Site notes:

Site name: _____

Web address: _____

Username: _____

C–D

Password	Date

Site notes:

Site name: _____

Web address: _____

Username: _____

C–D

Password	Date

Site notes:

Site name: _____

Web address: _____

Username: _____

C–D

Password	Date

Site notes:

Site name: _____

Web address: _____

Username: _____

Password	Date

E–F

Site notes:

Site name: _____

Web address: _____

Username: _____

Password	Date

E–F

Site notes:

Site name: _____

Web address: _____

Username: _____

Password	Date

E–F

Site notes:

Site name: _____

Web address: _____

Username: _____

E–F

Password	Date

Site notes:

Site name: _____

Web address: _____

Username: _____

Password	Date

E–F

Site notes:

Site name: _____

Web address: _____

Username: _____

Password	Date

E–F

Site notes:

Site name: _____

Web address: _____

Username: _____

Password	Date

E–F

Site notes:

Site name: _____

Web address: _____

Username: _____

Password	Date

E–F

Site notes:

Site name: _____

Web address: _____

Username: _____

Password	Date

G–H

Site notes:

Site name: _____

Web address: _____

Username: _____

Password	Date

G–H

Site notes:

Site name: _____

Web address: _____

Username: _____

Password	Date

G–H

Site notes:

Site name: _____

Web address: _____

Username: _____

G–H

Password	Date

Site notes:

Site name: _____

Web address: _____

Username: _____

Password	Date

G–H

Site notes:

Site name: _____

Web address: _____

Username: _____

Password	Date

G–H

Site notes:

Site name: _____

Web address: _____

Username: _____

Password	Date

G–H

Site notes:

Site name: _____

Web address: _____

Username: _____

Password	Date

G–H

Site notes:

Site name: _____

Web address: _____

Username: _____

Password	Date

I–J

Site notes:

Site name: _____

Web address: _____

Username: _____

Password	Date

I–J

Site notes:

Site name: _____

Web address: _____

Username: _____

Password	Date

I–J

Site notes:

Site name: _____

Web address: _____

Username: _____

Password	Date

I–J

Site notes:

Site name: _____

Web address: _____

Username: _____

Password	Date

I–J

Site notes:

Site name: _____

Web address: _____

Username: _____

Password	Date

I–J

Site notes:

Site name: _____

Web address: _____

Username: _____

Password	Date

I–J

Site notes:

Site name: _____

Web address: _____

Username: _____

Password	Date

I–J

Site notes:

Site name: _____

Web address: _____

Username: _____

Password	Date

K–L

Site notes:

Site name: _____

Web address: _____

Username: _____

Password	Date

K–L

Site notes:

Site name: _____

Web address: _____

Username: _____

Password	Date

K–L

Site notes:

Site name: _____

Web address: _____

Username: _____

Password	Date

K–L

Site notes:

Site name: _____

Web address: _____

Username: _____

Password	Date

K–L

Site notes:

Site name: _____

Web address: _____

Username: _____

Password	Date

K–L

Site notes:

Site name: _____

Web address: _____

Username: _____

Password	Date

K–L

Site notes:

Site name: _____

Web address: _____

Username: _____

Password	Date

K–L

Site notes:

Site name: _____

Web address: _____

Username: _____

Password	Date

M–N

Site notes:

Site name: _____

Web address: _____

Username: _____

Password	Date

M–N

Site notes:

Site name: _____

Web address: _____

Username: _____

Password	Date

M–N

Site notes:

Site name: _____

Web address: _____

Username: _____

Password	Date

M–N

Site notes:

Site name: _____

Web address: _____

Username: _____

Password	Date

M–N

Site notes:

Site name: _____

Web address: _____

Username: _____

Password	Date

M–N

Site notes:

Site name: _____

Web address: _____

Username: _____

Password	Date

M–N

Site notes:

Site name: _____

Web address: _____

Username: _____

Password	Date

M–N

Site notes:

Site name: _____

Web address: _____

Username: _____

Password	Date

O–P

Site notes:

Site name: _____

Web address: _____

Username: _____

Password	Date

O–P

Site notes:

Site name: _____

Web address: _____

Username: _____

Password	Date

O–P

Site notes:

Site name: _____

Web address: _____

Username: _____

Password	Date

O–P

Site notes:

Site name: _____

Web address: _____

Username: _____

Password	Date

O–P

Site notes:

Site name: _____

Web address: _____

Username: _____

Password	Date

O–P

Site notes:

Site name: _____

Web address: _____

Username: _____

Password	Date

O–P

Site notes:

Site name: _____

Web address: _____

Username: _____

Password	Date

O–P

Site notes:

Site name: _____

Web address: _____

Username: _____

Password	Date

Q–R

Site notes:

Site name: _____

Web address: _____

Username: _____

Password	Date

Q–R

Site notes:

Site name: _____

Web address: _____

Username: _____

Password	Date

Q–R

Site notes:

Site name: _____

Web address: _____

Username: _____

Password	Date

Q–R

Site notes:

Site name: _____

Web address: _____

Username: _____

Password	Date

Q–R

Site notes:

Site name: _____

Web address: _____

Username: _____

Password	Date

Q–R

Site notes:

Site name: _____

Web address: _____

Username: _____

Password	Date

Q–R

Site notes:

Site name: _____

Web address: _____

Username: _____

Password	Date

Q–R

Site notes:

Site name: _____

Web address: _____

Username: _____

Password	Date

S–T

Site notes:

Site name: _____

Web address: _____

Username: _____

Password	Date

S–T

Site notes:

Site name: _____

Web address: _____

Username: _____

Password	Date

S–T

Site notes:

Site name: _____

Web address: _____

Username: _____

Password	Date

S–T

Site notes:

Site name: _____

Web address: _____

Username: _____

Password	Date

S–T

Site notes:

Site name: _____

Web address: _____

Username: _____

Password	Date

S–T

Site notes:

Site name: _____

Web address: _____

Username: _____

Password	Date

S–T

Site notes:

Site name: _____

Web address: _____

Username: _____

Password	Date

S–T

Site notes:

Site name: _____

Web address: _____

Username: _____

Password	Date

Site notes:

U–V

Site name: _____

Web address: _____

Username: _____

Password	Date

U–V

Site notes:

Site name: _____

Web address: _____

Username: _____

Password	Date

Site notes:

U–V

Site name: _____

Web address: _____

Username: _____

Password	Date

U–V

Site notes:

Site name: _____

Web address: _____

Username: _____

Password	Date

Site notes:

U–V

Site name: _____

Web address: _____

Username: _____

Password	Date

U–V

Site notes:

Site name: _____

Web address: _____

Username: _____

Password	Date

Site notes:

U–V

Site name: _____

Web address: _____

Username: _____

Password	Date

U–V

Site notes:

Site name: _____

Web address: _____

Username: _____

Password	Date

Site notes:

W–X

Site name: _____

Web address: _____

Username: _____

Password	Date

Site notes:

W–X

Site name: _____

Web address: _____

Username: _____

Password	Date

Site notes:

W–X

Site name: _____

Web address: _____

Username: _____

Password	Date

Site notes:

W–X

Site name: _____

Web address: _____

Username: _____

Password	Date

Site notes:

W–X

Site name: _____

Web address: _____

Username: _____

Password	Date

Site notes:

W–X

Site name: _____

Web address: _____

Username: _____

Password	Date

Site notes:

W–X

Site name: _____

Web address: _____

Username: _____

Password	Date

Site notes:

W–X

Site name: _____

Web address: _____

Username: _____

Password	Date

Site notes:

Y–Z

Site name: _____

Web address: _____

Username: _____

Password	Date

Site notes:

Y–Z

Site name: _____

Web address: _____

Username: _____

Password	Date

Site notes:

Y–Z

Site name: _____

Web address: _____

Username: _____

Password	Date

Site notes:

Y–Z

Site name: _____

Web address: _____

Username: _____

Password	Date

Site notes:

Y–Z

Site name: _____

Web address: _____

Username: _____

Password	Date

Site notes:

Y–Z

Site name: _____

Web address: _____

Username: _____

Password	Date

Site notes:

Y–Z

Site name: _____

Web address: _____

Username: _____

Password	Date

Site notes:

Y–Z

Part III
Passwords Quick Reference

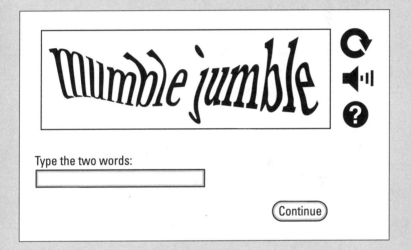

In this part . . .

*I*f an aphabetized directory isn't your style, how about a few simple pages where you can jot down the usernames and passwords for the accounts that are most important to you? In this part, you can record the login information for the accounts you use the most and access the info easily by flipping to the back of the book.

	Username	Password
Amazon:	_____	_____
Apple ID:	_____	_____
ATM:	_____	_____
Bank:	_____	_____
Credit card:	_____	_____
eBay:	_____	_____
E-Mail:	_____	_____
Facebook:	_____	_____
Google:	_____	_____
Home computer:	_____	_____
Investment account:	_____	_____
LinkedIn:	_____	_____
Microsoft account:	_____	_____
PayPal:	_____	_____
School account:	_____	_____
Smartphone:	_____	_____
Tablet:	_____	_____
Wi-Fi:	_____	_____
Work account:	_____	_____
Yahoo!:	_____	_____
_____:	_____	_____
_____:	_____	_____
_____:	_____	_____
_____:	_____	_____

	Username	Password
Amazon:		
Apple ID:		
ATM:		
Bank:		
Credit card:		
eBay:		
E-Mail:		
Facebook:		
Google:		
Home computer:		
Investment account:		
LinkedIn:		
Microsoft account:		
PayPal:		
School account:		
Smartphone:		
Tablet:		
Wi-Fi:		
Work account:		
Yahoo!:		
_____:		
_____:		
_____:		
_____:		

	Username	Password
Amazon:	_____	_____
Apple ID:	_____	_____
ATM:	_____	_____
Bank:	_____	_____
Credit card:	_____	_____
eBay:	_____	_____
E-Mail:	_____	_____
Facebook:	_____	_____
Google:	_____	_____
Home computer:	_____	_____
Investment account:	_____	_____
LinkedIn:	_____	_____
Microsoft account:	_____	_____
PayPal:	_____	_____
School account:	_____	_____
Smartphone:	_____	_____
Tablet:	_____	_____
Wi-Fi:	_____	_____
Work account:	_____	_____
Yahoo!:	_____	_____
_____**:**	_____	_____
_____**:**	_____	_____
_____**:**	_____	_____
_____**:**	_____	_____

	Username	Password
Amazon:		
Apple ID:		
ATM:		
Bank:		
Credit card:		
eBay:		
E-Mail:		
Facebook:		
Google:		
Home computer:		
Investment account:		
LinkedIn:		
Microsoft account:		
PayPal:		
School account:		
Smartphone:		
Tablet:		
Wi-Fi:		
Work account:		
Yahoo!:		
_____:		
_____:		
_____:		
_____:		

	Username	Password
Amazon:	_____	_____
Apple ID:	_____	_____
ATM:	_____	_____
Bank:	_____	_____
Credit card:	_____	_____
eBay:	_____	_____
E-Mail:	_____	_____
Facebook:	_____	_____
Google:	_____	_____
Home computer:	_____	_____
Investment account:	_____	_____
LinkedIn:	_____	_____
Microsoft account:	_____	_____
PayPal:	_____	_____
School account:	_____	_____
Smartphone:	_____	_____
Tablet:	_____	_____
Wi-Fi:	_____	_____
Work account:	_____	_____
Yahoo!:	_____	_____
_____:	_____	_____
_____:	_____	_____
_____:	_____	_____
_____:	_____	_____

	Username	Password
Amazon:	_____	_____
Apple ID:	_____	_____
ATM:	_____	_____
Bank:	_____	_____
Credit card:	_____	_____
eBay:	_____	_____
E-Mail:	_____	_____
Facebook:	_____	_____
Google:	_____	_____
Home computer:	_____	_____
Investment account:	_____	_____
LinkedIn:	_____	_____
Microsoft account:	_____	_____
PayPal:	_____	_____
School account:	_____	_____
Smartphone:	_____	_____
Tablet:	_____	_____
Wi-Fi:	_____	_____
Work account:	_____	_____
Yahoo!:	_____	_____
_____:	_____	_____
_____:	_____	_____
_____:	_____	_____
_____:	_____	_____

	Username	Password
Amazon:	_____	_____
Apple ID:	_____	_____
ATM:	_____	_____
Bank:	_____	_____
Credit card:	_____	_____
eBay:	_____	_____
E-Mail:	_____	_____
Facebook:	_____	_____
Google:	_____	_____
Home computer:	_____	_____
Investment account:	_____	_____
LinkedIn:	_____	_____
Microsoft account:	_____	_____
PayPal:	_____	_____
School account:	_____	_____
Smartphone:	_____	_____
Tablet:	_____	_____
Wi-Fi:	_____	_____
Work account:	_____	_____
Yahoo!:	_____	_____
_____:	_____	_____
_____:	_____	_____
_____:	_____	_____
_____:	_____	_____

	Username	Password
Amazon:	_____	_____
Apple ID:	_____	_____
ATM:	_____	_____
Bank:	_____	_____
Credit card:	_____	_____
eBay:	_____	_____
E-Mail:	_____	_____
Facebook:	_____	_____
Google:	_____	_____
Home computer:	_____	_____
Investment account:	_____	_____
LinkedIn:	_____	_____
Microsoft account:	_____	_____
PayPal:	_____	_____
School account:	_____	_____
Smartphone:	_____	_____
Tablet:	_____	_____
Wi-Fi:	_____	_____
Work account:	_____	_____
Yahoo!:	_____	_____
_____:	_____	_____
_____:	_____	_____
_____:	_____	_____
_____:	_____	_____

	Username	Password
Amazon:	_____	_____
Apple ID:	_____	_____
ATM:	_____	_____
Bank:	_____	_____
Credit card:	_____	_____
eBay:	_____	_____
E-Mail:	_____	_____
Facebook:	_____	_____
Google:	_____	_____
Home computer:	_____	_____
Investment account:	_____	_____
LinkedIn:	_____	_____
Microsoft account:	_____	_____
PayPal:	_____	_____
School account:	_____	_____
Smartphone:	_____	_____
Tablet:	_____	_____
Wi-Fi:	_____	_____
Work account:	_____	_____
Yahoo!:	_____	_____
_____:	_____	_____
_____:	_____	_____
_____:	_____	_____
_____:	_____	_____

	Username	Password
Amazon:	_____	_____
Apple ID:	_____	_____
ATM:	_____	_____
Bank:	_____	_____
Credit card:	_____	_____
eBay:	_____	_____
E-Mail:	_____	_____
Facebook:	_____	_____
Google:	_____	_____
Home computer:	_____	_____
Investment account:	_____	_____
LinkedIn:	_____	_____
Microsoft account:	_____	_____
PayPal:	_____	_____
School account:	_____	_____
Smartphone:	_____	_____
Tablet:	_____	_____
Wi-Fi:	_____	_____
Work account:	_____	_____
Yahoo!:	_____	_____
_____:	_____	_____
_____:	_____	_____
_____:	_____	_____
_____:	_____	_____

About the Author

Ryan C. Williams is a technical writer and author living in New Orleans, Louisiana. He has authored or coauthored such titles as *MySpace For Dummies, Google Business Solutions All-in-One For Dummies, Laptops Just the Steps For Dummies,* and *Teach Yourself Visually Bass Guitar* (a subject that takes up the rest of his time when he is not in front of a computer). His past experience includes providing technical support on both a professional and a "Can you help me with this?" family basis.

Dedication

To my wife Jennifer, who never fails to lift me out of the morass that spending too much time with computers can cause.

Author's Acknowledgments

Many thanks to the stellar Wiley editorial team that continues to tolerate me, including Steve Hayes, Heidi Unger, Amanda Graham, Annie Sullivan, Cherie Case, and the multitude of additional contributors to a project like this. Also, many thanks to the people who regularly and consistently maintain good security policies and don't share their passwords. You make life so much easier.

Publisher's Acknowledgments

Executive Editor: Steve Hayes

Project Editor: Heidi Unger

Copy Editor: Amanda Graham

Editorial Assistant: Annie Sullivan

Sr. Editorial Assistant: Cherie Case

Project Coordinator: Patrick Redmond

Cover Image: ©iStockphoto.com/JuSun